COPING WITH ANXIETY FOR KIDS

Effective Fun Strategies on Dealing with Stress,

Anxiety, and Anger Inside Your Children

Kenneth C. Hays

Other books by Kenneth C. Hays:

<u>Mastering Your Ego</u>

<u>Overcoming Overthinking</u>

<u>Giving Love A Second Chance</u>

<u>Who should make the first move?</u>

<u>Love Languages for Girls</u>

<u>Overcoming Avoidant Attachment Style</u>

Table of Contents

Introduction

Have you ever had that fluttery sensation in your gut when you're ready to do something new, like beginning a new school year or meeting someone for the first time? Well, that's entirely natural. It's a little thing we call anxiousness.

Anxiety is like an overprotective buddy who occasionally worries too much about you. It's not necessarily a negative thing, but occasionally it can become a little bossy, like a small dragon living in your mind.

But guess what? You're not alone in this quest! This book is your guide to understanding and taming that dragon. We're going to learn how to be the dragon whisperer — someone who can soothe their worry and make it a bit less fierce.

Lily was a bright and adventurous youngster, much like you. But there was one thing that made her pulse beat faster than a racing automobile — the dark and stormy evenings. Every time thunder rumbled and lightning flashed across the sky, Lily's worry dragon would wake up and start to growl. One day, Lily found something extraordinary. She unearthed a mysterious treasure box filled with extraordinary equipment and abilities to soothe her dragon. And that's what we're going to discover together in this book! Are you ready to find your own treasure vault of superpowers to conquer your worry dragon? Let's go on this amazing trip together. Remember, you're never alone in this, and you've got a world of support waiting for you!

In the pages that follow, we'll learn how to comprehend anxiety, detect its tactics, and employ fun and imaginative techniques to put it to sleep. So, let's flip the page and start this incredible discovery.

Chapter 1

Okay, my great buddy, let's start our adventure by studying what anxiety is. You may have heard grown-ups speak about it, but what does it imply for us kids?

Imagine you're ready to enter into a jungle, and you're not entirely sure what's hidden beneath those large, green leaves. That tingling sensation in your tummy, the quick pulse, or the way your palms grow a touch sweaty—that's worry saying hello! But don't worry, anxiousness is simply like a friendly alert system in your body. It's there to keep you safe and help you prepare ready for new and exciting activities. Sometimes, however, it might be a bit too enthusiastic and start buzzing when it's not essential.

Now, let me tell you a tale about Timmy.

Timmy was an adventurous adventurer. He liked going on excursions in his backyard, but one day, something weird occurred. He wanted to climb a tree, a large, tall one, and his heart began beating like a race car! "What's going on?" he pondered.

That's when Timmy's dad took him down and said, "You know, son, sometimes our bodies get a bit too enthusiastic, like when we're going to try something new. It's like our own personal alarm system, and it's called anxiety."

Timmy paused for a bit and remarked, "So, anxiety is like my body's superhero alarm?" His dad grinned and nodded, "Exactly, Timmy! It's there to safeguard you and make you ready for new experiences." And that's what we're going to learn more about in this chapter. We'll uncover how worry can be like a good buddy, and we'll find out how to detect when it's being a touch too cautious. So, let's get set to explore the world of anxiety together, much like Timmy on his travels in the garden!

Alright, courageous explorers, let's break down what anxiety is in a manner that's incredibly simple to understand:

Imagine you had a pal called "Worry Worm." Worry Worm loves to linger around in your head, and occasionally, it becomes a bit too talkative. It's like having a small voice that asks lots of questions and wants to make sure everything is good.

So, anxiety is like having your very own Worry Worm, and it's not a terrible thing! It's there to assist keep you safe and make sure you're ready for fun excursions. But occasionally, Worry Worm might speak a bit too much and start to worry about things that aren't a big concern.

Think of worry as Worry Worm's way of saying, "Hey, let's be careful and think about this!" So, when you experience that tingling sensation in your gut or those racing thoughts, it's simply your Worry Worm trying to be a wonderful buddy.

Understanding How Anxiety Feels

Anxiety may be a little like having a rollercoaster ride within you. Sometimes, worry makes your gut feel like a garden full of fluttery butterflies. It's like you're getting ready for something wonderful, but your butterflies are a bit too enthusiastic. It's like your heart is attempting to win a race! When anxiousness is present, your heart can beat quicker, like a drum in a parade. Imagine you're a leaf on a tree, and the wind is blowing. Anxiety might make you feel a bit wobbly or jittery, exactly like that leaf in the wind.

Sometimes, anxiousness brings loads of thoughts to the party. They can be ideas such as, "What if?" or "I'm not sure." It's like a giant thought parade in your mind. When anxiety arrives, it could make it hard to fall asleep or give you some strange nightmares. It's like your bedtime tale has a twist. Anxiety may sometimes make you ponder a lot about the future and what could happen. It's like a time traveler in your imagination.

Remember, all these sensations are like signals from your Worry Worm. They're here to aid you, and we'll learn how to comprehend them better in this quest. So, let's befriend our Worry Worm and learn to sail effortlessly over the rollercoaster of emotions.

Chapter 2: Identifying Anxiety

Common Triggers for Anxiety in Children

Now that we know what anxiety is, it's time to put on our detective hats and learn how to notice it when it attempts to creep in!

Picture this: You're on a treasure quest, and you're seeking secret clues. effectively, worry leaves hints too, but they're not buried very effectively. They're like beautiful feathers on a bird or footsteps on the sand.

Let's meet a new buddy, Mia.

Mia was an adventurous sailor. She liked going out on her boat and exploring the oceans. But occasionally, shortly before setting sail, her stomach would feel like it was performing cartwheels.

One day, Mia's granny joined her on the boat. She observed Mia's strange belly and inquired, "Mia, is there something you're excited about or maybe a little worried?" Mia paused for a bit and responded, "Well, Grandma, it happens when I'm about to go on a big adventure, like sailing." Grandma smiled and continued, "That sensation is like a communication from your body. It's saying, 'Hey, Mia, something major is occurring!' We call it anxiousness." Mia recognized that her body was providing her with these hints to let her know something huge was about to happen.

Recognizing Signs of Anxiety in Kids

Anxiety may often be like a cunning ninja, hidden in the shadows, making it tough to see. But don't worry; we're going to learn to detect its symptoms and uncover its mysteries. Here are some indications that might help you recognize anxiety in kids:

1. Tummy Troubles:.One classic indicator of anxiousness is when your gut feels like it's performing somersaults. You can feel nauseated, and that's your body's way of expressing, "Hey, something's up!"

2. Fast-Beating Heart: Just as when you play tag and your heart races, anxiety may make your heart beat quicker. It's like your body's way of screaming, "Get ready!"

3. Jitters and Shivers: If you ever feel a touch shaky or jittery, like a leaf in the wind, that may be anxiety attempting to gain your attention.

4. Sleepy or Restless Nights: Sometimes, worry may make it hard to fall asleep or give you weird nightmares. It's like a bedtime tale your body tells you, and it's saying, "We've got something to talk about."

5. Worry ideas: If your mind is loaded with loads of ideas that make you worry or feel uneasy, it's anxiety's method of knocking on the door of your thoughts.

6. Avoiding activities: When you start avoiding activities you used to love because they make you uneasy, that's an indication that anxiety could be attempting to play hide and seek.

7. Changes in Appetite: Anxiety may sometimes make you feel like eating a lot or

not eating much at all. It's like your body's way of expressing, "I'm feeling a bit different today."

Remember, it's good to experience these feelings; they're like messages from your body.

Common Triggers for Anxiety in Children Anxiety typically starts to crop up when something big or new is occurring.

Starting a new school, meeting new people, or attempting something you've never done before might make anxiety wake up and say, "What's going on?" Moving to a new house, parents going through a huge shift, or getting a new baby brother or sister may all stir up worry because things are changing. When there's a major test or exam at school, anxiety could try to help you prepare, but it might become a bit too eager.

Sometimes, thoughts about making friends or getting along with people might bring anxiety to the surface.

Things like thunderstorms, the dark, or frightening movies may also be triggers for anxiety, much like Mia and her boat excursions.

If your family is going through a stressful moment, such as money issues or health concerns, it might make anxiety want to be part of the discussion.

Chapter 3: Coping Strategies

Imagine you're on an expedition, and you're confronted with hurdles, like crossing a river or climbing a high hill. Coping methods are like items in your explorer's bag that assist you in conquering such problems. In this chapter, we'll find some fantastic methods to help us control our emotions and feel powerful, just like courageous explorers.

Breathing Exercises for Calm

Let's start with a magical ability you already have - your breath! Breathing exercises are like unique spells that help you calm down when your emotions are a little like a stormy sea. By taking steady, deep breaths, you may make the waves level out, and the sky in your mind becomes clear.

Imagine you're blowing up a balloon. Take a large, soft breath in through your nose, as you're smelling your favorite flower. Then, let the air out gently through your lips, like you're inflating up the balloon. As you do this, your belly rises and falls, much like the waves of the sea. It's like a tiny piece of magic you take with you wherever you go.

The Power of Positive Thinking

Now, let's speak about the power of your ideas. Positive thinking is like having a pair of magical glasses that enable you to see the sunny side of things, even on a foggy day. It's all about converting frowns into smiles!

Imagine your ideas are like seeds you grow in a garden. If you plant positive ideas, like "I can do it" or "I'm strong," your garden will be filled with lovely blooms. But if you plant negative beliefs, like "I can't" or "I'm not good enough," you'll have weeds in your garden.

So, we'll learn how to be gardeners of our ideas and make sure we're cultivating the most beautiful flowers in our brains. Positive thinking helps you believe in yourself and your talents.

Every adventurer needs a pleasant and secure place to relax, right? Creating a safe environment is like having your very own hidden retreat where you may feel peaceful and joyful. It's a location that's just for you, where you can be yourself.

Think of it as a treasure chest where you store all the things that make you feel secure and joyful. It may be your favorite blanket, a beloved cuddly animal, or a quiet place with your books. This safe area is like a warm embrace, a place where you may take a vacation from the outer world and find calm.

Expressing Emotions Through Art and Play

Sometimes, emotions are like bright paints, and art and play are your canvas. They provide you an opportunity to express your sentiments and let them out pleasantly and creatively. It's like having the ability to transmute emotions into beautiful paintings.

You may sketch, paint, construct with bricks, or even pretend to be a superhero in a world you design. It's a method to convey your sentiments without speaking a word, and it can be very, really enjoyable.

These tools will help us manage our emotions and be strong explorers, no matter what problems come our way.

Chapter 4: Mindfulness for Kids

Imagine you have a magical button inside you. When you press it, everything around you slows down, and you become a peaceful and happy explorer. This magical button is called mindfulness, and in this chapter, we'll learn how to use it to find calm in the middle of our adventures.

Practicing Mindfulness and Relaxation

Mindfulness is like a superpower that helps you focus on the here and now. It's about being fully present in the moment, like when you're savoring the taste of your favorite ice cream or feeling the warm sun on your face. It's like turning off the "worry switch" and letting happiness flow in.

One way to practice mindfulness is by taking a few deep, calming breaths. Imagine you're smelling a lovely flower and then blowing out a candle. These breaths help you calm the waves of your emotions and make you feel like a peaceful sea.

Another mindfulness trick is to imagine you're a statue. Stand or sit still like a statue and pay attention to your body, just like you're on a treasure hunt. You might notice how your toes feel in your shoes or the gentle rise and fall of your chest with each breath. This makes you feel like a calm and still pond.

Mindful Activities for Everyday Life

Mindful activities are like adventures in slow motion, where you pay close attention to what you're doing. It's like becoming a mindful detective and exploring the world around you with curious eyes and a happy heart.

Imagine you're eating a juicy, delicious apple. Instead of gobbling it up, you take small, mindful bites, noticing the taste, texture, and even the sound it makes when you chew. It's like turning an ordinary snack into a grand feast for your senses.

Chapter 5: Building Resilience

Think of resilience as a superpower that helps you bounce back from challenges, just like a rubber ball. It's like having a shield that makes you strong and brave. In this chapter, we'll learn how to be superheroes of resilience and face any adventure with courage!

Encouraging Problem-Solving

Imagine you're on a treasure hunt, and you come across a big, tricky puzzle. Problem-solving is like having a map and a flashlight to help you find your way through the puzzle.

When you face a challenge, it's like a riddle waiting to be solved. You can gather your thoughts and think of different ways to tackle it. It's like being a detective, exploring all the possible paths to success.

You might ask for help from trusted friends, like your sidekicks on this adventure, to find solutions together. It's like having a team of heroes on your side, working together to conquer any obstacle.

Dealing with Setbacks and Mistakes

Sometimes, adventures have unexpected twists, and you might make a wrong turn or a little mistake. But that's perfectly okay! Dealing with setbacks and mistakes is like having a magical eraser to fix things.

Imagine you're an artist, and your life is a big canvas. If you make a mistake while painting, you can simply paint over it with a new, colorful stroke. Mistakes are like opportunities to create something even more beautiful.

When you face a setback or make a mistake, it's like a plot twist in your adventure story. It doesn't mean the story is over; it means there's a chance for a new, exciting chapter. It's all part of the journey, making you wiser and more experienced.

Resilience is our secret power, helping us face every twist and turn with a fearless heart.

Chapter 6

Talking About Anxiety

Imagine that you had a treasure box full of emotions, and occasionally, these sentiments may seem a bit weighty. This chapter is like a roadmap to help you discuss such sentiments with your trusted grown-ups, like parents or caretakers. It's like having a specific key to unlock your treasure box and let those emotions out.

How to Share Feelings with Trusted Adults

Your sentiments are like bright diamonds in your treasure box, and expressing them with trustworthy grown-ups is like displaying them in your prized collection. It's crucial to realize that your emotions are meaningful and that your trusted adults are like guardians who want to listen and support you.

Imagine you have a great acquaintance called "Helper Owl." Helper Owl is always ready to listen and offer you a warm, loving embrace. Sharing your sentiments is like having a chat with Helper Owl. You may chat about what's on your mind, and Helper Owl will be there to console you.

When you reveal your sentiments, it's like opening up your treasure chest and letting some of the treasures sparkle in the light. Your trustworthy adults will be available to listen and give support. They want to help you feel better, exactly like mystical healers who have magical spells to make your troubles go.

Communicating with Parents and Caregivers

Parents and caregivers are like the commanders of your adventure ship. They steer you through the stormy waters and relish the beautiful days. Talking to them about your sentiments is like giving them a blueprint of your emotions.

Imagine you're a bold adventurer, and you've unearthed a message in a bottle. This message contains your sentiments, and you may pass it along to your parents or caretakers. They'll read it attentively and grasp what's on your heart.

It's crucial to realize that your trusted adults are like loving anchors. They'll listen to your emotions and assist you in navigating through any problems. When you chat with them, it's like navigating your ship into a safe port.

Chapter 7: Support from Family and Friends

Imagine you're part of a vast crew of explorers. This chapter is like a handbook to teach you how your family and friends are your teammates, and they're always ready to aid you on your trip through the ups and downs of life.

The Role of Parents in Helping Kids Cope

Parents are like the commanders of your adventure ship, bringing you through the seas and storms. They're there to listen, advise, and defend you. When you're feeling like you're sailing through turbulent waves, your parents may be like lighthouses, pointing you the route to safety.

Imagine you're a young adventurer, and your parents are your most trusted guides.

They comprehend the map of your emotions and know how to navigate the twists and turns of your journeys. When you share your sentiments with them, it's like sharing your treasure map. They'll help you locate the most valuable diamonds concealed in your heart.

Parents are like your greatest cheerleaders. They applaud your triumphs and help you learn from your setbacks. If you ever feel like you're lost in a dark jungle, they're like guides with a compass, bringing you back to the road of bravery and perseverance.

How Friends Can Be a Source of Support

Friends are like fellow travelers on the same path as you. They understand your enthusiasm and anxieties since they're going through comparable situations. Your pals may be like teammates, standing by your side while you're battling a monster or ascending a hard mountain.

Imagine you and your pals are like a squad of superheroes. You support each other and share your strengths. When one of you feels like they're in a deep jungle, the others may be like guides, helping you find your path and lending a hand when you stumble.

Friends may be like storytellers, sharing their own stories and the lessons they've learned. You may learn from one other's experiences and become stronger together. It's like having a giant book of tales that motivates you to be strong and confront obstacles head-on.

Chapter 8: The Importance of Self-Care

Self-care is all about how to make yourself feel joyful, calm, and powerful, just like a superhero who has to rest and recharge.

Teaching Kids to Take Care of Themselves

Taking care of oneself is like being the caretaker of your garden. It's about learning to listen to your emotions and needs. Imagine your heart is a smart buddy who informs you, "Hey, I need a little love and care today." That's when self-care comes in.

It's crucial to recognize that you are like a lovely flower in your garden, and self-care is like sunlight and rain that help you grow strong and healthy. Self-care teaches you to be nice to yourself, much like a compassionate gardener who waters the plants and offers them affection.

Parents and caregivers are like the assistants who guide you in the art of self-care. They teach you how to take care of your garden, and you may follow their example. It's like having a tutor who reveals the secret of how to make your garden blossom with delight.

Fun and Relaxing Self-Care Activities

Self-care activities are like fun for your heart and spirit. They are moments of delight and relaxation that help you feel peaceful and rejuvenated. Imagine you're a painter, and self-care activities are your colorful palette. You may select the colors that make you feel happiest.

You may enjoy a nice reading session with your favorite book, exactly like discovering a mystical world. It's like having an adventure in your imagination, where you can be a hero.

Or you can take a stroll in nature and feel the soil under your feet. It's like going into a fairy tale forest, where every step is a wonderful trip.

Self-care activities are like the magic wand that helps you shed any anxieties and make your heart sing with delight. They're like the gentle wind that clears the clouds and unveils the bright

You've learned that self-care is like a treasure trove of enjoyment and relaxation, waiting for you to uncover it. So, be nice to yourself and let your heart blossom with delight via self-care activities

Conclusion

Recap of Key Points

We've learned about anxiety, a friendly alarm system in our bodies, and how to recognize its colorful feathers. We've found the strong tools in our explorer's backpack, such as breathing exercises, positive thinking, and establishing a safe area. We've trained mindfulness to find tranquility and be present in the moment.

We've explored the assistance of our valued allies, family, and friends, who are always ready to lend a hand and listen. We've unlocked the power of self-care, taking care of our inner gardens, and nourishing our happiness and vigor.

As we complete our trip, remember that you are strong, brave, and capable of facing any problems that come your way. You have a treasure vault of resources, information, and support to assist you in negotiating the twists and turns of life.

Just like an adventurous explorer, your trip continues, and you may always return to this amazing realm anytime you need it. With a heart full of bravery and a mind packed with resilience, you're ready to tackle whatever road you choose.

So, keep exploring, keep learning, and keep developing. Your quest in "Coping with Anxiety for Kids" is a continuing journey, and you're the hero of your novel.